Viola (Removable Part) | Piano Accompaniment

A MUSICA...

EP...

INSTRUMENTAL SOLOS

Music by JOHN WILLIAMS

CONTENTS

© 2009 Alfred Publishing Co., Inc.
All Rights Reserved. Printed in USA.

Alfred

ISBN-10: 0-7390-5828-2
ISBN-13: 978-0-7390-5828-2

STAR WARS
(Main Theme)

Music by
JOHN WILLIAMS

Majestically, steady march (♩ = 108)

Star Wars - 5 - 1
32128

4

JAR JAR'S INTRODUCTION

By
JOHN WILLIAMS

Moderately (♩ = 80)

(Tempo click)

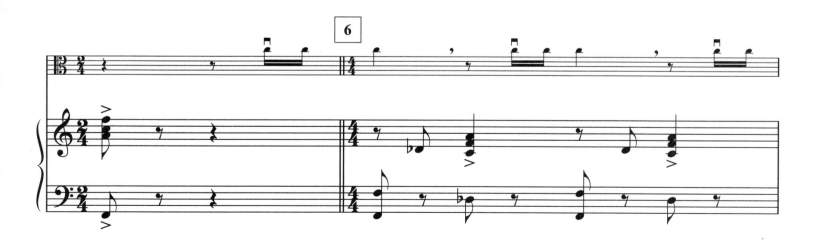

Jar Jar's Introduction - 3 - 1
32128

AUGIE'S GREAT MUNICIPAL BAND

By
JOHN WILLIAMS

Augie's Great Municipal Band - 4 - 1
32128

QUI-GON'S FUNERAL

By
JOHN WILLIAMS

Dirge, solemnly (♩ = 60)

(with pedal)

Qui-Gon's Funeral - 2 - 1
32128

DUEL OF THE FATES

Music by
JOHN WILLIAMS

Duel of the Fates - 8 - 1
32128

ANAKIN'S THEME

By
JOHN WILLIAMS

Moderato (♩ = 76)

Anakin's Theme - 4 - 1
32128

15

THE FLAG PARADE

By
JOHN WILLIAMS

Majestically (♩= 92)

(Tempo click)

The Flag Parade - 5 - 1
32128

THE ARENA

Music by
JOHN WILLIAMS

The Arena - 5 - 1
32128

ACROSS THE STARS
(Love Theme from *STAR WARS*®: EPISODE II)

Music by
JOHN WILLIAMS

Moderately slow & gently (♩ = 76)

(with pedal)

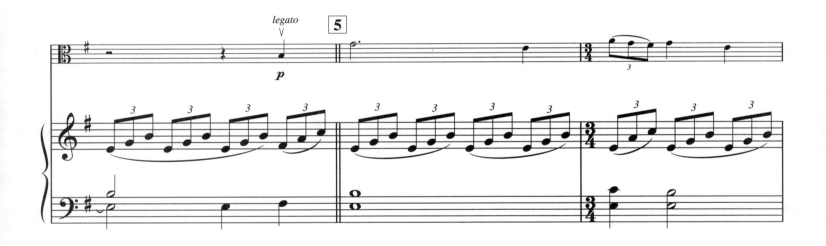

* The cue note represents a more challenging performance alternative.

THE MEADOW PICNIC

Music by
JOHN WILLIAMS

Moderately slow and flowing (♩. = 50)

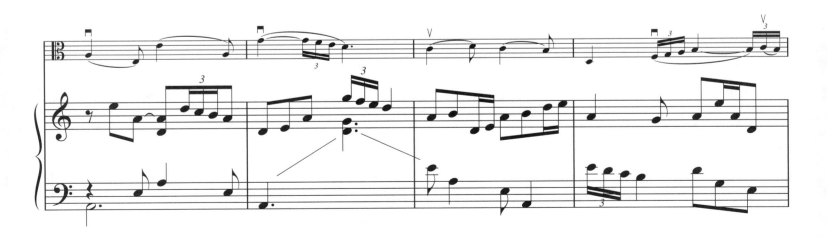

The Meadow Picnic - 3 - 1
32128

The Meadow Picnic - 3 - 2
32128

*E♯ = F♮

THE IMPERIAL MARCH
(Darth Vader's Theme)

Music by
JOHN WILLIAMS

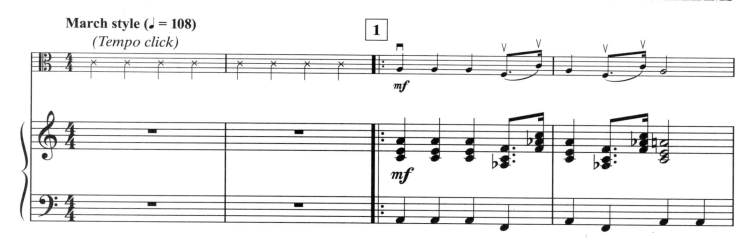

The Imperial March - 3 - 1
32128

20

BATTLE OF THE HEROES

(From *Star Wars*®: Episode III *Revenge of the Sith*)

Music by
JOHN WILLIAMS

CANTINA BAND

Music by
JOHN WILLIAMS

Moderately fast ragtime ($\quad$ = 112)

Cantina Band - 4 - 1
32128

To Coda ⊕

THE THRONE ROOM

Music by
JOHN WILLIAMS

*E♯ = F♮

**B♯ = C♮

The Throne Room - 4 - 1
32128

The Throne Room - 4 - 4
32128

MAY THE FORCE BE WITH YOU

Music by
JOHN WILLIAMS

(with pedal throughout)

May the Force Be With You - 3 - 1
32128

May the Force Be With You - 3 - 2
32128

PRINCESS LEIA'S THEME

Music by
JOHN WILLIAMS

Moderately slow, with a gentle flow (♩ = 72)

(with pedal)

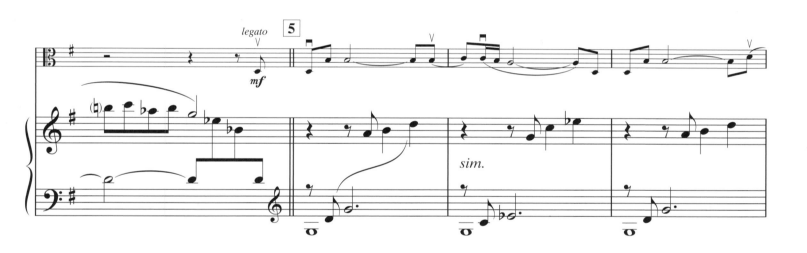

Princess Leia's Theme - 3 - 1
32128